Here
and
Now

Chiara Lubich

Here *and* Now

Meditations on Living in the Present

New City Press
Hyde Park, NY

Published in the United States by New City Press
202 Cardinal Rd., Hyde Park, NY 12538
www.newcitypress.com
©2005 New City Press

Newly translated from Italian (see Sources on p. 69)
Selections based on *Jeder Augenblick ist ein Geschenk*
©1996 Neue Stadt, Munich, Germany

Cover design by Durvanorte Correia

Library of Congress Cataloging-in-Publication Data:

Lubich, Chiara, 1920-
     [Selections. English. 2005]
   Here and now : meditations on living in the present / Chiara
                                    Lubich.--Pbk. ed.
      p. cm.
   ISBN 1-56548-232-8 (alk. paper)
    1. Meditations. 2. Christian life--Catholic authors. 3. Time--
Religious aspects--Christianity--Meditations. I. Title.

   BX2182.3 .L8313 2005
   242--dc22   2005013334

Printed in the United States of America

Contents

Living in the Present

Your Will Be Done

Rooted in Eternity

Foreword

What is time? We measure it, and we use it to measure an infinite number of things, music for one. We try to save it. We live in it. (Can we live without it?) Paul told us to redeem it. But we have to admit that we do not perfectly understand what it means. Has it real existence of its own? Or is it something we have made up as an aid to measuring the sequence and duration of events or to describing historical incidents in relation to each other? Even for the greatest scientists it is hard to define; it remains to some extent a mystery — one of the most fascinating.

There are lots of good ways to spend time: books to read from which we have much to learn, letters to answer, people to call, and places it would be good to visit, like Lourdes or the Holy Land or, for health purposes, Florida or the dentist's office. But we don't have time for many of them.

Our time is limited. That is reality. Consequently, hardly anything is more important to us than to use what time we have as well as possible. There is no sense in wasting it. If we do not accept our time limits, we will feel miserably frustrated. There is no need for that. Let us live in reality and enjoy it, and let go of what we cannot have, like the moments of the past. We can enjoy some memories and learn from them, but we cannot live in them. Like footprints washed away in the sand, they are gone. Failings we regret are gone too; God has forgiven them.

As for the future, it does not yet exist. So, let us free ourselves from anxiety about it. The best way to prepare for it, in a sense the only way, is the use of the one time element of which none of us has less or more than anyone else, the present moment. For this, that, or the other thing we might not have time, but *we do have the here and now*. We all have an equal share. It cannot be increased or diminished. And we do not know for sure how many moments we'll be given. But we have this one, and it's a great gift, precious in the extreme, and unique.

Our own time is limited, but the present moment is the way to be connected with what is *un*limited and outside of time: eternity. Augustine explained this very convincingly. The Creator of time is outside of time. God lives in a never-ending present, what Augustine called a *nunc stans*, a 'now-standing-still', a point with no beginning and no end, with no past or future, where everything is 'now'. All goodness and reality that could ever be is in him. Our connection with it is in the present. Augustine says that living in the love of God in the present moment puts us already in heaven. This is the height of realism.

We cannot live in each other's time and place. For one of us in America it may be Saturday afternoon, for another in Asia it is Sunday morning at the same moment. For one of us, says the Book of Ecclesiastes, it may be the time to weep; for others, a time to laugh. There is a time to plant, and a time to root up; a time to lie down and a time to get up. Everything in creation has its time and place.

In the light of her Christian faith and a lifetime of experience with her friends, Chiara Lubich gives us advice on how to use well the 'here and now'. In another place at some future time we might have a good influence, but it is likely to be in proportion to how well we are using this particular moment, infinitesimal though it may be. If we focus on the present moment, we are planting a seed in eternity, to be enjoyed forever.

Julian Stead, O.S.B.
Author of *Saint Benedict*
A Rule for Beginners

Living in the Present

Don't Look Back

Always look ahead, never back. What has happened in your life has happened, and God knows it. Now only one thing matters: not to miss the present moment, the only thing we really have in our hands. Only in the present can we love God with all our heart and do his will.

When We Live
the Present Moment

When we live the present moment we can fulfil all our duties
. . . our crosses become bearable (that is why this practice is advised to those who are approaching death)
. . . we understand God's voice within
. . . the strength of his grace works in us
. . . we can succeed in reaching holiness
. . . and we will find ourselves at the evening of each day, and at the evening of our life, rich in good works and acts of charity.

When Evening Comes ...

If we fully live the present moment, then we find a sense of dignity about all we do, however small it may be.

When evening comes, we remember these fully lived moments with joy. And should we become aware of imperfections, we entrust these to God whose mercy can correct them.

With this view of life, examining our conscience in the evening becomes much easier. It gains importance and becomes as significant as the exam at the close of our earthly life, in a certain sense even more so. Because, while at the end of our life there is no further remedy, after our daily examination we can try again and take the exam once more the next day, if God gives us the chance.

Then, we can even accept the suffering that our imperfections of passed days brought us and make it bear fruit.

'Little' Things

> 'Anyone who is trustworthy in little
> things is trustworthy in great.'
> (Lk 16:10)

Scripture teaches us to do little things well. This becomes a marked characteristic of persons who do wholeheartedly what God asks of them in the present.

If we live in the present, God lives in us. And if God is in us, then charity is in us. Those who live in the present are patient, persevering, gentle, detached in all things, pure, and merciful. Love lives in them in its highest and most genuine expression. They truly love God with all their heart, soul, and strength. They are inwardly illuminated and guided by the Holy Spirit; so they do not judge or think badly of others but love their neighbours as themselves. They are strong enough to 'offer the other cheek' and to 'go two miles' (Mt 5:41) — that is, to live the evangelical 'foolishness'.

Often they find an opportunity to give to Caesar what is Caesar's (cf. Mt 22:21), because they also strive to carry out their duties as true citizens. . . .

Whoever lives the present is on the *way* of Christ, in his *life* and in his *truth*. This is what completely satisfies the soul, which longs for fullness at all times of its life.

What Counts is
How We Do Things

What counts for us Christians is not how *much* we do, but *how* we do it.

The historical Jesus did not change the world either. On the contrary, sometimes he seemed to fail.

What matters is to fulfil the plan God has for us — no more, but also no less.

Wherever we are, let us work adoring his will, which binds us to the present moment. This helps us to take care, one detail at a time, of what we need to achieve in the world.

If we move about like separate pieces, disunited, we will feel like we are achieving next to nothing. But if we are united, we will see that what one of us does is connected with what the others are doing. Then all our doing acquires fullness and a new dimension. A dimension which is not just universal but heavenly, since compared to heaven the universe is small.

Let us place love then into everything: the smiles we give, the jobs we do, the car we drive, the meal we prepare, the activity we organize, the tear we shed for Christ in our suffering neighbour, the instrument we play, the article or letter we write, the happy event we joyfully share, the clothes we clean . . .

Everything, really *everything* can become a means to show God and neighbour our love. All has been entrusted into our hands and hearts so that like missionaries we may bring the gospel to the world.

A Note of Dignity

If people begin — or begin again — to live the present moment well, you will notice with time that their actions have taken on a note of dignity, even if they didn't set out to do so. You can see that person's only and supernatural support: love for God.

This festive note, which characterizes such persons' every action, gives colour to their lives. As a consequence, their inner lives gain ever more focus.

Many things can be said of them: in prayer they are immersed in God, in company free and cheerful, in their duties precise, with themselves demanding; towards everyone they are like a brother or sister, with those in their care exacting; they are merciful with those who fall and convinced of their own nothingness and God's all powerfulness; often dissatisfied with their own accomplishments, they are always ready to hope and begin again.

It is precisely this consistent beginning again which is a great help to us, who are weakened by original sin. It gives us a sense of continuity, even as we do a great variety of things. It gives a sense of holiness, little at first, but then more and more.

Because holy is the one who lives no longer in self, in the will of the self, but is transferred instead into the will of Another.

Christ, Our Way

We will never fully understand the value of living in the present moment. Let it suffice to say that this is the attitude that experienced spiritual teachers recommend to people who are dying.

If I live in the present, God is with me in his will, present to me with his grace. Otherwise, he is far from me and I from him.

We often strive to find ways that will lead us to him. We want to become better, even become saints. But why look for ways if he is *the* way (cf. Jn 14:6)? He is ever present and waiting to work together with us in each moment of our life. In the time given us, he wants to enable us to accomplish things worthy of God's children.

Sometimes we want to change this quiet and dull way of life. We want to go against the current of the world and return to the pure heights of the divine. And we feel that trials, heavy blows, sufferings, mortifications, and agonies might help us attain this.

What we can be sure of is that God reveals himself in the present — in the painful and inevitable circumstances of life as well as in our conscious self-denials to which Christ calls us in many ways: 'Deny yourself and take up your cross' (Mt 16:24).

Life can be so simple if we don't complicate it! It is enough to be rooted in the present with all its joys, surprises, efforts, and commitments. Everything will run smoothly as though we were carried by a powerful force toward the beatitude of eternity.

Letting Ourselves
Be Carried

When we walk, we have to use our own strength, and we move quite slowly.

If we use a bicycle, we move not only faster but also with less effort. Some of our limbs are practically at rest.

Although pilots fly planes at high speeds, their own effort is minimal. The engines do most of the work.

In space flight, astronauts work still less compared to the technical work of their space capsules.

The same is true for our spiritual life. The closer we get to God, the more we are carried by him. Until there is nothing left to do but to allow ourselves to be carried. Our effort will mostly consist in this.

Today Has Troubles Enough

> 'So do not worry about tomorrow:
> tomorrow will take care of itself.
> Each day has enough trouble of its own.'
> (Mt 6:34)

God is generous in everything. But when it comes to suffering, the Lord says, 'Each day has enough trouble of its own.'

We know that he does not deceive us. So if we follow his will and concern ourselves only with today's troubles, the worries we were expecting tomorrow may never actually happen.

Our Daily Cross

When we live the present moment, and live it well, we realize that we are always able to live out Christ's words, 'Take up your cross' (cf. Mt 16:24). Almost every moment has its cross. Tiny, small, and greater spiritual or physical sufferings always accompany our lives. We have to 'take up' these crosses, not try to avoid them by escaping into an uncommitted lifestyle.

And even when we are healthy and joyful, we do well not only to thank God for all this, but also to live detached from it all, and not cling to the gift rather than to the Giver. Otherwise we will find ourselves sad and empty.

In God's Hand

O ften we are tormented by thoughts of what the future might hold. But, 'Each day has enough trouble of its own' (Mt 6:34). Tomorrow is another day, and we shall then face tomorrow's troubles.

We don't need to worry; everything is in God's hands. He will allow only his will to be accomplished, and this is always for our good.

Life

J oy and sorrow
hope,
dreams come true.
Maturity of life and thought.
Solidity.
Sense of duty,
the call of love from above
answered
by the coherence of our life.
Weariness.
Flames and conquests.
Storms.
Trust in God:
God alone.
Peaks.
Valleys.
Torrential downpours,
deep roots.
Fruits, fruits, fruits . . .
Clouding of the soul:

'My God, my God . . .'
Then sweet music from heaven,
in the distance at first.
Then nearer.
Drum rolls:
Victory!

The road of life,
long and varied,
but the goal is near.
All,
every single thing,
has,
has always had,
one sole destiny:
union with You.

To Begin Again

To begin again. This is the thought which should guide my whole day.

It is not when everything is fine that things are going well. It is when — sad or joyful, in good health or not — we offer everything to the Lord, trying to be another him.

Paul writes: 'I do not reckon myself as having taken hold of it; I can only say that forgetting all that lies behind me, and straining forward to what lies in front, I am racing towards the finishing-point to win the prize of God's heavenly call in Christ Jesus' (Ph 3:13-14).

A wonderful sentence. We must grasp the depth of each word. There are people who do forget the past, but they do not push on ahead; they don't even think about the finish line. Others forget the past and keep beginning again. But to forget and then push on with enthusiasm to the finish line is typical of a saintly person like Paul.

But what can stop us from trying to do the same?

Time Will not Wait...

Catherine of Siena used to say: 'Don't wait for time . . . because time won't wait for you.' Like many other sayings, this is one sentence we should never forget. Let us love God in the present moment, doing his will with all our heart.

Your Will
Be Done

The Time
that Remains

'How quickly time passes,' we exclaim, as we watch in bewilderment the days flying by.

'How time remains!' we would say if we consciously spent every hour and every moment completely in fulfilling your will.

Working
in Perfect Communion

It is wise to spend the time we have by living God's will to the full in the present moment.

Sometimes, however, we worry about the past or the future. We are concerned about situations or people for whom we cannot do anything at the moment.

This is when it becomes difficult to steer the ship of our lives. It takes great effort to keep to the course that God wishes us to have in that particular moment. At such times we need strong willpower, determination, and especially trust in God, sometimes to a heroic degree.

Can I do nothing to resolve a certain complex situation or for a dear person who is sick or in danger? Then I will concentrate on doing well what God wants from me in the present: study, homemaking, prayer, taking care of the children . . . God will take care of the rest. He will comfort the suffering and show a way out of that entangled situation.

This way the task is being done by two in perfect communion. It demands from us great faith in God's love for his children. And in turn it gives God a chance to trust that we do our part. This mutual trust works miracles. We will realize that Another has accomplished what we could not do, and that he has done it far better than we could have.

Then our trust will be rewarded. Our limited life acquires a new dimension: we feel near the infinite for which we yearn. Our faith invigorates and gives our love new strength. We will know loneliness no longer. Since we have experienced it, we will be more deeply aware of being children of a God, who is a Father and who can do everything.

Be Vigilant

In order to love God we need to do his will. But his will presents itself one moment at a time.

It may be expressed by external circumstances, by our own duties, by some advice from more experienced people. . . . Or even by unexpected events, be these sorrowful or delightful, annoying or indifferent.

God's will can be understood only by one who is attentive and vigilant. This is why the gospel speaks so often of vigilance.

The gospel directs us toward the present. It tells us not to worry about the future, to ask the Father only for our *daily* bread. Jesus invites us to carry *today's* cross and says that *each* day has trouble enough of its own. And he warns us that 'Once the hand is laid on the plough, no one who looks back is fit for the kingdom of God' (Lk 9:62).

To get used to living the present well, we Christians must know how to forget the past and how not to worry about the future. This is only common sense: after all, the past exists no more and the future will be when it becomes present. Catherine of Siena said: 'The fatigue of the past we don't have, because time has gone by. The fatigue of the future we don't have either, because we can't be sure that we will have that time.'

Great persons and saints know this principle. They are used to discerning God's voice from among the various inner voices. And with practice it becomes easier, also because God's voice becomes stronger and is amplified.

At the start it might be more difficult. First we need to learn how to trust in God, to believe in his love, and to do with determination what we think is his will. We can be confident that he will bring us back on track, should we end up going astray. And even when God's will seems to be clear, calling us for example to do a job that will take hours, there is always a temptation to overcome, a scruple to be driven away, some worry to be entrusted to the heart of God, wandering thoughts to get away from, desires to say no to.

Living the present is a practice that is extraordinarily rich. It grafts our earthly life already now into eternity.

The Compass

O n a plane trip a few years ago, a kind
stewardess invited me into the cockpit.
I was impressed by the magnificent view,
wide and unobstructed, offered by the large
cockpit windows, but even more so by the
pilot's explanations.

To steer the airplane, he told me, you
must first set the compass needle in the
direction of your destination. Then, along
the way, you must keep an eye on it to make
sure that the plane does not go off course.

In my mind I began to compare an airplane trip with the journey of our life, which
we also call our 'holy journey'. Here, too, we
have to start by setting our 'compass' in the
direction our soul is to follow: Jesus who
cries on the cross, 'My God, my God, why
have you forsaken me?' On the way we have
to do only one thing: remain faithful to him.

This is the path God calls us to follow: to love Jesus forsaken in every suffering we encounter in our lives. This means adhering to his will out of love, putting aside our own will so as to let his prevail. To love Jesus forsaken means to discover what true love is, to learn how to love our neighbours the way he loved us. It means to practise all the virtues just as in that moment he heroically did. . . .

On that plane I noticed that the pilot could move about freely. He didn't need reins as you would need with a horse or a steering wheel as you would with a car. If we set the needle of our spiritual compass in the direction of Jesus forsaken, we too will not need anything else to reach our goal safely.

On a plane trip there are no curves to take you by surprise because you fly in a straight line, and you don't have the problem of mountains because you quickly reach a high altitude. On our holy journey, our love for Jesus forsaken immediately places us at a good altitude. Thus we are not frightened by unforeseen circumstances, nor tired out by climbing. Whatever is unforeseen, difficult, or painful has already been foreseen and expected in Jesus forsaken.

When we get up in the morning, let's set our compass on Jesus forsaken ... and during the day, from time to time, let's check if we are still on the right course. If we realize that we are not, we promise him again our fidelity.

This way, we too will be able to repeat with Saint Clare: 'Go, confidently, my soul, because you have a good companion for your journey. Go, because the one who has created you, has always watched over you, and has sanctified you.'

Rooted in God

Instead of *living* our lives, we often simply
skim the surface.

Help us, Lord, to be rooted in you in every
instant, by being moment by moment
rooted in your divine will.

The Train of Time

At the beginning of our community, the Focolare, we were in constant danger of losing our lives, because we were not adequately sheltered during the air raids. So when the question arose as to when we had to do God's will in order to love him, we immediately understood that the answer was: now — right now. For we did not know if we would still be alive later.

The only time in our possession was the present moment. The past was already gone, and we did not know if the future would ever come. We used to say: the past no longer exists; let's entrust it to God's mercy. The future is not yet here. By living the present, we will also live the future well when it becomes present.

We realized how foolish it was to live in the past, which will never return, or in the future, which may never come and which, in any case, is unpredictable.

We took the example of riding on a train. Just as a traveller remains seated and would not think of walking up and down the aisle in order to get to the destination sooner, so we had to remain in the present. The train of time moves ahead on its own.

Living the present, one moment after another, we will one day reach that decisive moment upon which our eternity depends. Having loved *God's will* in the present with all our heart, all our soul, all our strength, we will have fulfilled throughout our lives the commandment to love *God* with all our heart, all our soul, all our strength.

Becoming Saints

Souls are often attracted by the idea of sanctity. Maybe it is actually the grace of God at work, stirring up such a desire in them.

Thinking about the preciousness of saints, of the influence of their personalities on their times, of the widespread and ongoing revolution that they have brought to the world, is often what kindles the flame of this yearning. But at times the soul so sweetly tormented by this idea looks to the saints as if confronted with an insuperable chasm or an impenetrable wall.

'What could I do to become a saint?' the soul asks.

'What test, what system, what practices, what ways to follow are there?'

'If I knew that penance would do it, I would scourge myself from dawn to dusk. If I knew that it takes prayer, I would pray night and day. If it were sufficient to be a preacher, I would love to go through the cities and villages, giving myself no rest to bring God's word to everybody . . . but I don't know, I simply don't know the way.'

Every saint has features of his or her own, and saints look as different from one another as the greatest variety of flowers in a garden. . . .

But maybe there is a way which is good for everyone.

Maybe we do not need to figure out our own way, nor draw up plans or dream up a programme; instead, plunge ourselves into the fleeting moment to fulfil for that instant the wish of him who called himself 'the Way' (Jn 14:6), the best of ways. The past moment exists no longer; the next shall perhaps never be ours. But it is certain that we can love God in the moment granted us at present. Holiness is built in time.

Nobody knows their own holiness; often not another person's either, so long as we are alive. It is only when the soul has completed its course and taken its exam, that it reveals to the world what was God's plan for it.

Our task then is to build holiness moment by moment, responding with all our heart, soul, and strength to the love God bears us — a love that is personal as our heavenly Father and as great as the love of a God.

Your Will Be Done

For who does not love God very much, but to some extent fears him, the words 'Your will be done' have a ring of resignation about them. Who instead truly and sincerely loves God understands that God's will is the greatest and most exalted thing to do.

Nothing could be greater than to follow such a Father, who guides us moment by moment, speaking to us in many different ways. He speaks to us through the circumstances of life, through teachings, our duties, inspirations, suffering, through things that happen and through precepts and laws. All of these are like notes of a melody, which is composed in heaven and played on earth by the compliant harp of a heart in love with God.

God, who loves each and every one with an infinite love, has prepared for all of us a varied and divine adventure. Sacred and profane, tragic and nostalgic, feasting and mourning, form in it a stupendous painting, which we will understand better in the next life when we see everything in God's glorious light.

Rooted

in

Eternity

In Solidarity with All

Sometimes it seems that a life of faith lived consistently — that is, in view of the life to come and in expectation of death, its doorway — somewhat detaches us from the concerns of the world. We Christians are sometimes blamed for being too little committed to the interests of this world, which often represent the good of humanity.

In reality, though, if we always live in the awareness of knowing 'neither the day nor the hour' we concentrate more easily on the 'today' which we have been given, on today's troubles, on the present moment which God gives us. With all our being we can live in the present and accept whatever it brings us: joy and sorrow, effort and results. This is how we truly *live* our life on this earth.

On the contrary, without the awareness that sooner or later we have to depart from this life, we might lead a superficial existence based on illusions, dreams, and on things we are aiming at but perhaps never achieve.

Living the present, therefore, does not lead us to forget the earthly future or to clip the wings of planning for our own good and that of others like our children and family, the community we live in, and humanity. Neither does it make us forget the past with its heritage of thoughts, heroism, and conquests.

We can only be true Christians if we have in our hearts love toward all people. This is our nature and prerogative. Being children of God, Christians share in love *par excellence*, the same love Christ has for the Father.

Christians know that they are a part of humanity, like small tiles of a marvelous mosaic in the making. Their love goes out to the humanity of the past, the present, and the future.

They approach the heritage of past generations with the respect of those who know that it has been entrusted to them, with the humility of who has to learn from it, and with the awareness that they must transmit it to future generations, enriched by their own commitment.

If Christians realize in their lives that God wants them to think of tomorrow, they do so with complete commitment, not for themselves but out of love for those who will come after them, whether they know them or not.

This consciousness of being one with all of humanity, past, present, and future, this love for others as for oneself, is for Christians the driving force that makes them fit and strong for building today what will be a better future tomorrow.

It is precisely the one who lives in view of the next life and lives this earthly life accordingly, with a love for all, who becomes a perfect Christian and a fulfilled person. This is not only what our times and our humanity is waiting for, but above all what God is expecting from us.

Works that Last

If you live the present, and live it well, you accomplish works that last, even if you may speak to only one person or to only one category of people. Meeting just one person or group, you encounter all of humanity. Just as doing one specific task well, you fulfil all of God's will. Experiencing this totally satisfies you, because you embrace infinity.

This means doing well in the present what God wants, and doing it *as* God wants it to be done, according to his system and his dynamics. If, for example, you prepare a talk to be given in public, do so with all of the Holy Spirit's help within you. Then propose it to your friends in an atmosphere of mutual love. Be humble and ready to 'lose' your proposal so that it may 'die', decay, and be reborn from unity. . . . This way your words will remain and bear fruit. And what otherwise might do some good to one person and then be lost, will do good to many and continue to do so.

Living the present in this way gives a sense of fullness, because it is in harmony with Jesus' life within us. He in us achieves works that remain.

If then you realize that you have not done your part well or only partially, entrust it to the heart of Jesus with great confidence. Be aware that any moment can be the last (and that we might have to leave behind us things done imperfectly). But know that Jesus desires only to love you and in concrete ways. He is ready to fill in what is lacking, to forgive your mistakes and to hide them from others. Just like a mother would do, and even more!

So even in this case you can rest assured: everything is done; everything fulfilled.

The True Meaning
of Time

There are times in our life in which we treasure every moment. For example, we might anxiously follow every move and glance, every word and longing, of a loved one close to eternal life. We value this final passage of life, because we are before death. Eternity, in fact, gives true meaning to time.

Maybe we should treasure every moment of our life in this way. We should seize the present moment, live it in love for God, and thus make it eternal.

Keep Your Eyes Open

'Stay awake,
because you do not know
either the day or the hour.'
(Mt 25:13)

Sometimes God urges us to live in a constant 'supernatural' attitude. When we live in absolute uncertainty as regards plans, journeys, our health and our future, we return to the only thing that is truly real: living the present moment before God, knowing and willing only what God would have us know and will. This is why we need to be watchful, as Jesus has commanded us, since we know neither the day nor the hour of his coming — of his *every* coming, we might add.

He always comes, in each moment, in his will, which may appear either sad or beautiful to our eyes, but in which we always encounter God himself, his love.

Being watchful means that we have our feet on the ground, the 'ground' of the heavenly kingdom, which we can and should experience already in this life. On this ground, there is no danger of falling into sin, illusions, delusions or anxiety.

A Day without Evening

Every day passes by and evening comes quickly.

Before my hour comes, Lord, accept my life, accept each moment that is still ahead of me.

I don't know why, but sometimes a sense of dissatisfaction sours moments of my life. Maybe because I need to be entirely uprooted by you, to the last root which might still tie me down to who knows what, and is not completely lost in you.

Maybe life is supposed to be like this: a constant journey. We rest in the illusion of an order that life occasionally promises and which we inadvertently long for. But as soon as we reach it, it already risks boring us.

You always did your daily duties well. But even you, up to the age of thirty, looked beyond to the mission that was ahead of you. And when you started your public life, those three brief years were a constant running.

You spent them on the road, gathering disciples, healing the sick, sowing the word, enamoring people. It was the quick moving of Wisdom, which as you grew in age built the Kingdom of God ever more quickly.

And you reached Calvary almost without realizing it. You passed through it in a few hours, giving body and soul to God for us.

Maybe our incapacity to hold on to the escaping moment, always reaching the evening too fast, is a drop of your life here on earth in us.

Thank you, Jesus, for life. Prepare us to die well and bring us with you, to the place where the sun never sets.

The Home
We Build Here

Life is an important transition: it is a test! As much of Jesus as I allow to be built up within me will be set for ever in the other life. Every moment, my every act and breath have their reflection in eternal life! Every minute of my life down here influences Life! 'Paradise is a home we build here but inhabit in the other life.'

As If It Were
the Last Day

Lord,
Help me to say every word
as if it were my last.
Help me to carry out every deed
as if it were my last act.
Help me to suffer always
as if it were the last suffering I have
to offer to you.
Help me to pray always
as if it were the last chance
I have here on earth
to speak to you.

Our Daily Bread

'Give us today our daily bread.'
(Mt 6:11)

Today. You really want us to live *your* way, Lord!

But who in our world lives like this, in the 'today', only for 'today'? Who abandons themselves to the future like free-flying birds for whom you provide food and clothes?

Living only for 'today' simplifies but also frightens our human nature. We would like to build on a secure future. Yet, there may not be a tomorrow. . . .

You, Lord, want us to be watchful. You announce another kingdom to which we will be called on a day and at an hour unknown to us. You are right, and you cannot contradict yourself.

Give us the grace, therefore, to live well for the rest of our life each day you give us.

Sources

The selected texts in this book have been taken and newly translated from the following works by Chiara Lubich, all published by Città Nuova, Rome (numbers refer to page numbers in this book, followed by the page number in the Italian original):

Scritti spirituali/1 (L'attrattiva del tempo moderno), 1991:
13:137; 25:234; 27:261; 31:236; 35:238; 42:238f; 45-46:94f; 47:237; 56:129; 58-59:147f; 60:127

Scritti spirituali/2 (L'essenziale di oggi), 1984:
15:101; 16-17:100; 18-19:215f; 20-21:214; 22-23:93f; 24:230; 26:201; 28-29:195; 36-37:208f; 38-39:121ff; 51-53:202f; 54-55:114f; 57:27; 62:109

Scritti spirituali/4 (Dio è vicino), 1995:
43-44:238f

In cammino col Risorto, 1994: 14:159f

La vita, un viaggio, 1994: 40-41:142ff

Città Nuova (magazine), XVIII, March 25, 1974: 61:25

Diario 1964/65, 1985: 30:150

NEW CITY PRESS
www.newcitypress.com
1-800-462-5980

Thank you for choosing this book.
If you would like to receive regular information
about New City Press titles, please fill in this card.

Title purchased:—————————————

Please check the subjects that are of particular interest to you:

- ○ **FATHERS OF THE CHURCH**
- ○ **CLASSICS IN SPIRITUALITY**
- ○ **CONTEMPORARY SPIRITUALITY**
- ○ **THEOLOGY**
- ○ **SCRIPTURE AND COMMENTARIES**
- ○ **FAMILY LIFE**
- ○ **BIOGRAPHY / HISTORY**
- ○ **INSPIRATION / GIFT**

Other subjects of interest: —————————————

(please print)

Name: —————————————————

Address: —————————————————

—————————————————

Telephone: —————————————————

New City Press
202 Cardinal Rd.
Hyde Park, NY 12538

Place
Stamp
Here